This book

Children's
POOLBEG

First published 1989 by
Poolbeg Press Ltd.
Knocksedan House,
Swords, Co. Dublin, Ireland.

© Introduction and Selection
Sean McMahon 1989

This book is published with the assistance of
The Arts Council/An Chomhairle Ealaíon, Ireland.

ISBN 1 85371 046 6

Cover design by Steven Hope
Typeset by Print-Forme,
62 Santry Close, Dublin 9.
Printed by The Guernsey Press Ltd.,
Vale, Guernsey, Channel Islands.

"Shoes and ships
and sealing-wax"

"Shoes and ships and sealing-wax"

Edited by
Sean McMahon

Children's
POOLBEG

For Ruairi and Conor

Introduction

People are fond of quotations. They are forever saying, "Shakespeare said ... " or "It says in the Bible ... " or even, when they don't quite know and are too lazy to look it up, "As the poet says ... " And no wonder! People in the past have said some things very well and these sayings have often an elegance and a succinctness that most of us can never attain. We have the thoughts but not always the knack of putting them neatly into words. As Pope says (you can see how catching it is!) "What oft was thought but ne'er so well expressed."

This book is for young people, a term I would not attempt to define except to say that you are creatures not quite adult, and I hope it will be used in the same way as the many other books of quotations that keep on being printed. A good phrase or a couple of lines of verse come into the head and stay there and we naturally wonder, "Who said that?" Or for an essay, or a speech, or for an argument in a debate you might want to find a nice remark that somebody with a way with words once made about your topic—life, death, politics, love, shoes, ships even. So you look up the index and find something which advances your case or perhaps, to your dismay, something that confounds your argument. Or again, you may enjoy leafing through this book to find what the famous have said in the past. In some cases you may find that some very smart things were said by people who are only famous because they said them. You will also find some very funny things which you can try out on your friends.

Shoes and Ships and Sealing-Wax (and if you don't know where that quotation came from, use the index to find out) can serve as a ever-present help (another quotation?) with your own writing and speaking. It is also a pleasant book to open and find something really neat in when you are tired or bored. It's good crack and trouble-free, like toast with the burnt crusts cut off or meat with the nasty gristle and bones removed. Enjoy!

Thomas Ady c. 1655

1.1   Matthew, Mark, Luke and John,
The bed be blest that I lie on.
Four angels to my bed,
Four angels round my head,
One to watch, and one to pray,
And two to bear my soul away.

'A Cradle in the Dark' (1655)

Aesop 6th century

1.2   I am sure the grapes are sour.

Fables 'The Fox and the Grapes'

1.3   While I see many hoof-marks going in, I see
none coming out.

'The Lion, the Fox, and the Beasts'

1

2.1   Don't count your chickens before they are hatched.

'The Milkmaid and her Pail'

2.2   The boy cried 'Wolf, wolf!' and the villagers came out to help him.

'The Shepherd's Boy'

2.3   The lamb that belonged to the sheep whose skin the wolf was wearing began to follow the wolf in the sheep's clothing.

'The Wolf in the Sheep's Clothing'

Louisa May Alcott 1832-1888

2.4   'Nicely, thank you, Mr Laurence; but I am not Miss March, I'm only Jo,' returned the young lady.

Little Women

Cecil Frances Alexander 1818-1895

2.5   All things bright and beautiful,
All creatures great and small,
All things wise and wonderful
The Lord God made them all.

'All Things Bright and Beautiful'

2.6   There is a green hill far away,
Without a city wall,
Where the dear Lord was crucified,
Who died to save us all.

'There is a Green Hill'

William Allingham 1828-1889

3.1   Up the airy mountain,
     Down the rushy glen,
     We daren't go a-hunting,
     For fear of little men.

'The Fairies'

3.2   Four ducks on a pond,
     A grass bank beyond,
     A blue sky of spring,
     White clouds on the wing:
     What a little thing
     To remember for years ...
     To remember with tears!

'A Memory'

St Ambrose 337-397

3.3   Si fueris Romae, Romano vivito more;
     Si fueris alibi, vivito sicut ibi.
     When in Rome live as the Romans do;
     When elsewhere, live as they live elsewhere.

Advice to St Augustine (Attrib.)

Hans Christian Andersen 1805-1875

3.4   'But the Emperor has nothing on at all!' cried
     a little child.

'The Emperor's New Clothes'

Anonymous

4.1 Whenever you see the hearse go by
And think to yourself you're gonna die,
Be merry, my friends, be merry.

Your eyes fall in and your hair falls out
And your brains come tumbling down your
    snout,
Be merry, my friends, be merry.

'Be Merry'

4.2 Jack o' the lantern, Joan the wad!
Who tickled the maid and made her mad,
Light me home, the weather's bad.

'Charm on seeing a Pisky'

4.3 'Who killed Cock Robin?'
'I', said the Sparrow
'With my bow and arrow,
I killed Cock Robin!'

'Cock Robin'

4.4 Come lasses and lads, get leave of your dads,
And away to the Maypole hie,
For every he has got a she,
And the fiddler's standing by.

'Come Lasses and Lads'

5.1   The common cormorant or shag
Lays eggs inside a paper bag.
The reason you will see no doubt
Is to keep the lightning out.
But what these unobservant birds
Have never noticed is that herds
O' wandering bears may come with buns
And steal the bags to hold the crumbs.

'The Common Cormorant'

5.2   Me father was the keeper of the Eddystone
    Light,
He married a mer-my-aid one night;
Out of the match came children three—
Two was fish and the other was me.

'The Eddystone Light'

5.3   What a wonderful bird the frog are—
When he sit he stand almost;
When he hop, he fly almost.
He ain't got no sense hardly;
He ain't got no tail hardly either,
When he sit, he sit on what he ain't got—
    almost.

'The Frog'

5.4   I'll tell my ma when I get home,
The boys won't leave the girls alone
They pull my hair they stole my comb,
But that's all right till I go home.

'I'll Tell My Ma'

6.1   How many miles to Babylon?
Three score and ten.
Can I get there by candle-light?
Yes and back again.

'A Lifetime'

6.2   Lizzie Borden took an axe
And gave her mother forty whacks;
And when she saw what she had done
She gave her father forty-one.

(Lizzie Borden was acquitted of murdering her father
and step-mother on 4 August 1892 in F all River, Mass.)

'Lizzie Borden'

6.3   And you'll tak' the high road and I"ll tak' the
low road,
And I'll be in Scotland afore ye;
But me and my true love will never meet
again
On the bonnie, bonnie banks o' Loch Lomond

'Loch Lomond'

6.4   Monday's child is fair of face,
Tuesday's child is full of grace,
Wednesday's child is full of woe,
Thursday's child has far to go,
Friday's child is loving and giving
Saturday's child works hard for a living,
And the child that is born on the Sabbath day
Is bonny and blithe and good and gay.

'Monday's Child'

7.1   I know a funny little man,
As quiet as a mouse,
Who does the mischief that is done
In everybody's house
There's no one ever sees his face,
And yet we all agree
That every plate we break was cracked
By Mr Nobody.

'Mr Nobody'

7.2   My Aunt Jane, she took me in.
She gave me tea out o' her wee tin
Half a bap and a wee snow top
And cinnamon buds out o' her wee shop.

'My Aunt Jane'

7.3   Old Mother Hubbard
Went to the cupboard
To give the poor dog a bone;
When she came there
The cupboard was bare
And so the poor dog had none.

'Old Mother Hubbard'

7.4   A swarm of bees in May
Is worth a load of hay;
A swarm of bees in June
Is worth a silver spoon;
A swarm of bees in July
Is not worth a fly.

Old Saying

8.1   I and Pangur Ban, my cat,
      'Tis a like task we are at;
      Hunting mice is his delight
      Hunting words I sit all night.

                              'Pangur Ban' (trans. Robin Flower)

8.2   I like little pussy, her coat is so warm;
      And if I don't hurt her, she'll do me no harm.
      So I'll not pull her tail, nor drive her away,
      But pussy and I very gently will play.
      She shall sit by my side, and I'll give her some
      food;
      And she'll love me because I am gentle and
      good.

                                                  'Pussy'

8.3   The man in the wilderness said to me,
      How many strawberries grow in the sea?
      I answered him as I thought good,
      As many red herrings as grow in the wood.

                                              'A Riddle'

8.4   Simple Simon met a pieman
      Going to the fair;
      Said Simple Simon to the pieman
      'Let me taste your ware,'

                                          'Simple Simon'

9.1 Der Spring is sprung
Der grass is riz
I wonder where dem boidies is?

Der little boids is on der wing,
Ain't dat absoid?
Der little wings is on der boid!

'Spring in Noo York'

9.2 Sumer is icumen in.
Lhude sing cuccu!
Groweth sed and bloweth med
And springth the wude nu.

'Sumer is icumen in'

Archimides 287-212

9.3 Eureka! (I have found it!)

On discovering his Principle

9.4 Give me a firm spot on which to stand, and I will move the earth.

On the Lever

Neil A. Armstrong 1930-

9.5 That's one small step for a man, one giant leap for mankind.

On landing on the moon, 21 July 1969

Jane Austen 1775-1817

9.6 An egg boiled very soft is not unwholesome.

Emma

10.1 It is a truth universally acknowledged, that a single man in possession of a good fortune, must be in want of a wife.

Pride and Prejudice

Alfred Austin 1835-1913

10.2 Across the wires the electric message came: 'He is no better, he is much the same.'

On the Illness of the Prince of Wales

The Rev W. Awdry

10.3 'You've got a lot to learn about trucks, little Thomas. They are silly and must be kept in their place.' said the Fat Controller, smiling. 'After pushing them about here for a few weeks you'll know almost as much about them as Edward. Then you'll be a Really Useful Engine.'

Thomas and the Trucks

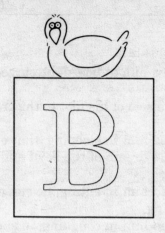

Francis Bacon 1561-1626

11.1 Studies serve for delight, for ornament, and for ability.

11.2 Some books are to be tasted, others to be swallowed, and some few to be chewed and digested.

11.3 Reading maketh a full man; conference a ready man and writing an exact man.

Of Studies

Edward Bangs fl. 1775

11.4 Yankee Doodle came to town
Riding on a pony;
Stuck a feather in his cap
And called it macaroni.

'Yankee Doodle'

R H Barham 1788-1845

12.1 He cursed him at board, he cursed him in
      bed;
      From the sole of his foot to the crown of his
      head;
      He cursed him in sleeping, that every night
      He should dream of the devil and wake in a
      fright;
      He cursed him in eating, he cursed him in
      drinking,
      He cursed him in coughing, in sneezing, in
      winking;
      He cursed him in sitting, in standing, in
      lying;
      He cursed him in walking, in riding, in
      flying;
      He cursed him in living, he cursed him in
      dying!

The Jackdaw of Rheims, from *The Ingoldsby Legends*

Sabine Baring-Gould 1834-1924

12.2 Onward, Christian soldiers,
      Marching as to war,
      With the Cross of Jesus
      Going on before.

'Onward, Christian Soldiers'

Phineas T Barnum (American Showman) 1810-1891

12.3 There's a sucker born every minute.

Attrib.

James Matthew Barrie 1860-1937

13.1 When the first baby laughed for the first time, the laugh broke into a thousand pieces and they all went skipping about and that was the beginning of fairies.

Peter Pan

13.2 To die will be an awfully big adventure.

Ib

13.3 Do you believe in fairies? ... If you believe, clap your hands!

Ib

13.4 Oh the gladness of her gladness when she's glad,
And the sadness of her sadness when she's sad,
But the gladness of her gladness
And the sadness of her sadness
Are as nothing, Charles,
To the badness of her badness when she's bad.

Rosalind

Max Beerbohm 1872-1956

13.5 To give an accurate and exhaustive account of that period would need a far less brilliant pen than mine.

Diminuendo

Brendan Behan 1924-1964

14.1 So many belonging to me lay buried in
     Kilbarrack, the healthiest graveyard in
     Ireland, they said, because it was so near the
     sea.

                                                      Borstal Boy

14.2 A hungry feeling came o'er me stealing
     And the mice were squealing in my prison
        cell,
     And that old triangle
     Went jingle jangle,
     Along the banks of the Royal Canal.

                                                The Quare Fellow

Hilaire Belloc 1870-1953

14.3 Child! do not throw this book about;
     Refrain from the unholy pleasure
     Of cutting all the pictures out!
     Preserve it as your chiefest treasure.

                              Bad Child's Book of Beasts, dedication.

14.4 The chief defect of Henry King
     Was chewing little bits of string

                                    Cautionary Tales: 'Henry King'

14.5 Matilda told such dreadful lies
     it made one Gasp and Stretch one's Eyes.

                                               Ib. 'Matilda'

15.1 The Devil, having nothing else to do,
Went off to tempt my Lady Poltigrue.
My Lady, tempted by a private whim,
To his extreme annoyance tempted him.

Epigrams 'On Lady Poltigrue, a Public Peril.'

15.2 When I am dead, I hope it may be said:
'His sins were scarlet, but his books were
read.'

Ib. 'On his Books'

15.3 Do you remember an Inn,
Miranda?

'Tarantella'

E(dmund) C(lerihew) Bentley 1875-1956

15.4 The art of Biography
Is different from Geography.
Geography is about maps,
But Biography is about chaps.

'Biography for Beginners'

15.5 Sir Humphrey Davy
Abominated gravy.
He lived in the odium
Of having discovered Sodium.

Ib.

15.6 Sir Christopher Wren
Said, 'I am going to dine with some men.
If anyone calls
Say I am designing St Paul's.'

'Josh Billings' (Henry Wheeler Shaw) 1818-1885

16.1 The wheel that squeaks the loudest is the
      one that gets the grease.

'The Kicker'

Col. William Blacker 1777-1855

16.2 He comes, the open rebel fierce—he comes
         the Jesuit sly;
      But put your trust in God, my boys, and
         keep your powder dry.

Oliver Cromwell's Advice

James W Blake 1862-1935

16.3 East side, West side, All around the town,
      The tots sing 'Ring-a-Rosie, London Bridge
         is falling down';
      Boys and girls together, me and Mamie
         O'Rourke,
      Trip the light fantastic on the sidewalks of
         New York

'The Sidewalks of New York'

William Blake 1757-1827

16.4 A Robin Redbreast in a cage
      Puts all Heaven in a Rage.

'Auguries of Innocence'

16.5 Bring me my bow of burning gold!
      Bring me my arrows of desire
      Bring me my spear! O clouds, unfold!
      Bring me my chariot of fire!

Milton, preface

17.1 I will not cease from Mental Fight
Nor shall my Sword sleep in my hand,
Till we have built Jerusalem.
In England's green and pleasant Land.

Ib.

17.2 Tyger! Tyger! burning bright
In the forests of the night,
What immortal hand or eye
Could frame thy fearful symmetry?

Songs of Experience: 'The Tyger'

17.3 Little Lamb, who made thee?
Dost thou know who made thee?
Gave thee life and bade thee feed,
By the stream and o'er the mead;

Ib. 'The Lamb'

17.4 When the green woods laugh with the voice
of joy,
And the dimpling stream runs laughing by;
When the air does laugh with our merry
wit,
And the green hill laughs with the noise of
it.

'Laughing Song'

Francis William Bourdillon 1852-1921

17.5 The night has a thousand eyes,
And the day but one.

'Light'

Charles, Baron Bowen 1835-1894

18.1 The rain it raineth on the just
And also on the unjust fella:
But chiefly on the just, because
The unjust steals the just's umbrella.

Attrib.

William Boyle 1853-1922

18.2 You're like Lanna Macree's dog—a piece of
the road with everybody.

The Eloquent Dempsey

Rupert Brooke 1887-1915

18.3 Here tulips bloom as they are told;
Unkempt about those hedges blows
An English unofficial rose.

'The Old Vicarage, Grantchester'

18.4 For Cambridge people rarely smile,
Being urban, squat, and packed with guile.

Ib.

18.5 Stands the Church clock at ten to three?
And is there honey still for tea?

Ib.

18.6 If I should die, think only this of me:
That there's some corner of a foreign field
That is for ever England.

'The Soldier'

Phillips Brooks 1835-1893

19.1 O little town of Bethlehem,
How still we see thee lie;

'O Little Town of Bethlehem'

Lord Brougham 1778-1868

19.2 Education makes a people easy to lead but
difficult to drive;
easy to govern but impossible to enslave.

Attrib.

Robert Browning 1812-1892

19.3 That's the wise thrush; he sings each song
twice over,
Lest you should think he never could
recapture
The first fine careless rapture!

'Home Thoughts from Abroad

19.4 Just for a handful of silver he left us,
Just for a riband to stick to his coat.

'The Lost Leader'

John Bunyan 1628-1688

19.5 So he passed over, and all the trumpets
sounded for him on the other side.

The Pilgrim's Progress

Gelett Burgess 1866-1951

20.1 I never saw a purple cow,
I hope I never see one;
But, I can tell you, anyhow,
I'd rather see than be one.

'The Purple Cow'

Dean John William Burgon 1813-1888

20.2 Match me such marvel, save in Eastern
    clime,
A rose-red city 'half as old as Time!'

'Petra'

Edmund Burke 1729-1797

20.3 It is the nature of all greatness not to be
exact.

American Taxation

20.4 It is now sixteen or seventeen years since I
saw the Queen of France, then the
Dauphiness, at Versailles; and surely never
lighted upon this orb, which she hardly
seemed to touch, a more delightful vision.

Reflections on the Revolution in France

20.5 But the age of chivalry is gone. That of
sophisters, economists and calculators has
succeeded; and the glory of Europe is
extinguished for ever.

Ib.

Robert Burns 1759-1796

21.1 Gin a body meet a body
       Coming through the rye;
       Gin a body kiss a body,
       Need a body cry?

'Coming Through the Rye'

21.2 Flow gently, Sweet Afton, among thy green
       braes
       Flow gently, I'll sing thee a song in thy
       praise.
       My Mary's asleep by thy murmuring
       stream,
       Flow gently, sweet Afton, disturb not her
       dream.

'Flow Gently, Sweet Afton'

21.3 Green grow the rashes O,
       Green grow the rashes O:
       The sweetest hours that e'er I spend
       Are spent amang the lasses O!

'Green Grow the Rashes'

21.4 O wad some Pow'r the giftie gie us
       To see oursels as other see us!

'To a Louse'

21.5 The best laid schemes o' mice and men
       Gang aft a-gley.

'To a Mouse'

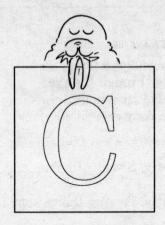

Julius Caesar 102-44 BC

22.1 Gallia est omnis divisa in partes tres.
(The whole of Gaul is divided into three parts)

De Bello Gallico

22.2 Et tu, Brute?

(Alleged dying words)

22.3 Iacta alea est.
(The die is cast)
(At the crossing of the Rubicon river)

Attrib.

22.4 Veni, vidi, vici.
(I came, I saw, I conquered)

Attrib.

William Camden 1551-1623

23.1 My friend judge not me,
Thou seest I judge not thee,
Betwixt the stirrup and the ground
Mercy I asked, mercy I found.

'Epitaph for a Man Killed by Falling from his Horse.'

'Ethna Carbery' (Anna MacManus) 1866-1902

23.2 They come with vengeance in their eyes
Too late, too late are they
For Rody McCorley goes to die
On the bridge of Toome today.

'Rody McCorley'

Henry Carey 1693-1743

23.3 Of all the girls that are so smart
There's none like pretty Sally,
She is the darling of my heart
And she lives in our alley.

'Sally in our Alley'

Francis Carlin 1861-1925

23.4 On Douglas Bridge I met a man
Who lived adjacent to Strabane,
Before the English hung him high
For riding with O'Hanlon.

'Ballad of Douglas Bridge'

Julia A Carney 1823-1908

24.1 Little drops of water,
    Little grains of sand
Make the mighty ocean
    And the beauteous land.

'Little Things'

24.2 And the little moments,
    Humble thought they be,
Make the mighty ages
    Of eternity.

Ib.

Lewis Carroll 1832-1898 **[Charles Lutwidge Dodgson]**

'24.3 'Curiouser and curiouser!' cried Alice.

Alice in Wonderland

24.4 You are old, Father William,' the young
    man said,
'And your hair has become very white;
And yet you incessantly stand on your
head—
Do you think at your age it is right?'

'In my youth,' Father William replied to his
    son.
'I feared it might injure the brain;
But now that I'm perfectly sure I have none,
Why, I do it again and again.'

Ib.

25.1 Twinkle, twinkle, little bat!
How I wonder what you're at!
Up above the world you fly
Like a tea-tray in the sky.

Ib. (The Mad Hatter)

25.2 Speak roughly to your little boy,
And beat him when he sneezes;
He only does it to annoy,
Because he knows it teases.

Ib.

25.3 'It was the *best* butter,' the March Hare
meekly replied.

25.4 'Twas brillig, and the slithy toves
Did gyre and gimble in the wabe;
And mimsy were the borogoves,
And the mome raths outgrabe.

Through the Looking-Glass

25.5 Now *here*, you see, it takes all the running
You can do, to keep in the same place.

Ib. (The Red Queen)

25.6 Tweedledum and Tweedledee
Agreed to have a battle;
For Tweedledum said Tweedledee
Had spoiled his nice new rattle.

Ib.

26.1 'The time has come,' the Walrus said,
     'To talk of many things:
Of shoes—and—ships—and sealing wax—
     Of cabbages and kings—
And why the sea is boiling hot—
     And whether pigs have wings.'

Ib.

26.2 When *I* use a word,' Humpty Dumpty said in a rather scornful tone, 'it means just what I choose it to mean—neither more nor less.'

Ib.

John Keegan Casey 1846-1870

26.3 Out from many a mud-wall cabin
Eyes were watching thro' that night,
Many a manly chest was throbbing
For the blessed warning light.
Murmurs passed along the valley
Like the banshee's lonely croon,
And a thousand blades were flashing
At the risin' of the moon.

'The Rising of the Moon' A.D. 1798

Patrick Reginald Chalmers 1874-1942

26.4 What's lost upon the roundabouts we pulls up on the swings.

'Green Days and Blue Days: Roundabouts and Swings'

Neville Chamberlain 1869-1940

27.1　I believe it is peace for our time ... peace with
honour.

> Wireless speech after Munich Agreement, 1 October 1938

Raymond Chandler 1888-1959

27.2　Down these mean streets a man must go who
is not himself mean; who is neither tarnished
nor afraid.

> *The Simple Art of Murder*

Emperor Charles V 1500-1558

27.3　I speak Spanish to God, Italian to women,
French to men, and German to my horse.

> *Attrib.*

Geoffrey Chaucer 1328-1400

27.4　Whanne that Aprille with his shoures sote
The droghte of Marche has perced to the
rote.

> *The Canterbury Tales*: 'The Prologue'

G(ilbert) K(eith) Chesterton 1874-1936

27.5　For the great Gaels of Ireland
　　　Are the men that God made mad,
For all their wars are merry,
　　　And all their songs are sad.

> 'Ballad of the White Horse'

28.1 My friends, we will not go again or ape an
 ancient rage,
 Or stretch the folly of our youth to be the
 shame of age,
 But walk with clearer eyes and ears this
 path that wandereth,
 And see undrugged in evening light the
 decent inn of death;

'The Rolling English Road'

Lord Randolph Churchill 1849-1894

28.2 Ulster will fight; Ulster will be right.

Letter, 7 May 1886

Sir Winston Churchill 1874-1964

28.3 We shall defend our island, whatever the cost
 may be, we shall fight on the beaches, we
 shall fight on the landing grounds, we shall
 fight in the fields and in the streets, we shall
 fight in the hills; we shall never surrender.

Speech, 4 June 1940

28.4 Let us therefore brace ourselves to our
 duties, and so bear ourselves that, if the
 British Empire and its Commonwealth last
 for a thousand years, men will still say, 'This
 was their finest hour.'

Speech, 18 June 1940

29.1 Never in the field of human conflict was so much owed by so many to so few

Speech about the RAF in the Battle of Britain, 20 August 1940

Colley Cibber 1671-1757

29.2 O say! What is that thing called Light,
   Which I can ne'er enjoy.

'The Blind Boy'

29.3 Whilst thus I sing, I am a King,
   Altho' a poor blind boy.

Ib.

Will D Cobb 1876-1930

29.4 School-days, school-days, dear old golden
      rule days,
   Readin' and 'rithin' and 'rithmetic,
   Taught to the tune of a hick'ry stick.

'School-Days'

Frank Colby 1865-1925

29.5 Men will confess to treason, murder, arson,
   false teeth or a wig. How many of them will
   own up to a lack of humour?

Essays

Samuel Taylor Coleridge 1772-1834

30.1 Water, water, everywhere,
And all the boards did shrink;
Water, water, everywhere.
Nor any drop to drink.

'The Ancient Mariner'

Padraic Colum 1881-1972

30.2 O, men from the fields!
Come gently within.
Tread softly, softly,
O, men coming in.

'A Cradle Song'

30.3 Och! but I'm weary of mist and dark,
And roads where there's never a house or
bush!

'An Old Woman of the Roads'

William Congreve 1670-1729

30.4 Music hath charms to soothe a savage breast,
To soften rocks, or bend a knotted oak.

The Mourning Bride

30.5 Oh fie Miss, you must not kiss and tell.

Love for Love

Emperor Constantine 288-337

30.6 In hoc signo vinces
(Beneath this sign you will conquer)

Heard in a vision of the Cross

James Fenimore Cooper 1789-1927
31.1 The Last of the Mohicans

Title of Novel

John Wilson Croker 1780-1857
31.2 A game which a sharper once played with a
dupe, entitled, 'Heads I win, tails you lose.'

Croker Papers

Oliver Cromwell 1599-1658
31.3 Remark all these roughnesses, pimples,
warts and everything as you see me, other-
wise I will never pay a farthing for it.

Instruction to Lely, on the painting of his portrait.

Charles Anderson Dana 1819-1897

32.1 When a dog bites a man that is not news, but when a man bites a dog that is news.

What is News

Dante Alighieri 1265-1321

32.2 Nel mezzo del cammin di nostra vita
(In the mid-course of our life)

Divina Commedia: 'Inferno'

32.3 Lasciate ogni speranza voi ch'entrate
(All hope abandon, ye who enter here)

Ib.

Thomas Davis 1814-1845

33.1 And Ireland long a province be
A Nation once again!

'A Nation Once Again'

33.2 But sure the great God never planned
For slumbering slaves, a home so grand.

'The West's Asleep'

Stephen Decatur 1779-1820

33.3 Our country! In her intercourse with foreign
nations, may she always be in the right; but
our country, right or wrong.

Toast given at Norfolk, Virginia, April 1816.

John De Courcy d. 1219

33.4 In burgo Duno tumulo; tumulantur in uno
Brigida, Patricius, atque Columba Pius.
(In Down three saints one grave do fill,
Brigid, Patrick and Colmcille)

Attrib.

Daniel Defoe 1661-1731

33.5 It happened one day, about noon, going towards my boat, I was exceedingly surprised
with the print of a man's naked foot on the
shore, which was very plain to be seen on the
sand. I stood like one thunderstruck, or as if I
had seen an apparition.

The Life and Adventures of Robinson Crusoe

34.1 I takes my man Friday with me.

Ib.

34.2 Wherever God erects a house of prayer,
The Devil always builds a chapel there;
And 'twill be found upon examination
The latter has the largest congregation

The True-Born Englishman

Antonin, Duc De Lauzun 1633-1723

34.3 It is unnecessary for the English to bring
cannon to such a place as this. What you call
ramparts might be battered down with
roasted apples.

Before Limerick, 20 July 1690

Augustus De Morgan 1806-1871

34.4 Great fleas have little fleas upon their backs
to bite 'em,
And little fleas have lesser fleas, and so ad
infinitum.

A Budget of Paradoxes

John Dennis 1657-1734

34.5 Damn them! they will not let my play run,
but they steal my thunder!

(on hearing his stage effects used by another dramatist)

Charles Dickens 1812-1870

35.1 'God bless us everyone!' said Tiny Tim, the last of all.

A Christmas Carol

35.2 Annual income twenty pounds, annual expenditure nineteen nineteen six, result happiness. Annual income twenty pounds, annual expenditure twenty pounds ought and six, result misery (Mr Micawber).

David Copperfield

35.3 Oliver Twist has asked for more! (Mr Bumble)

Oliver Twist

35.4 'If the law supposes that,' said Mr Bumble ... 'the law is a ass—a idiot.'

Ib.

35.5 I wants to make your flesh creep. (The Fat Boy)

Pickwick Papers

35.6 It is a far, far better thing that I do, than I have ever done; it is a far, far better rest that I go to, than I ever ever known.

A Tale of Two Cities

Henry Dixon 1675-1760

36.1 The boy that is good,
Does learn his book well;
And if he can't read,
Will strive for to spell.

'The Description of a Good Boy'

36.2 His school he does love,
And when he is there,
For play and for toys,
No time can he spare.

Ib.

Sir Arthur Conan Doyle 1859-1930

36.3 You know my methods, Watson.

The Crooked Man

36.4 'Excellent!" I cried. 'Elementary,' said he.

Ib.

36.5 'Is there any other point to which you would
wish to draw my attention?'
'To the curious incident of the dog in the
night-time.'
'The dog did nothing in the night-time.'
'That was the curious incident,' remarked
Sherlock Holmes.

Silver Blaze

37.1 Said the King to the Colonel:
'The complaints are eternal
That you Irish give more trouble
Than any other corps.'

The Irish Colonel

37.2 Said the Colonel to the King:
'This complaint is no new thing,
For your foemen, Sire, have made it
A hundred times before.'

Ib.

Lady Helen Selina Dufferin 1807-1867

37.3 I'm sittin' on the stile, Mary,
Where we sat side by side.

'Lament of the Irish Emigrant'

Alexander Dumas 1803-1870

37.4 All for one, one for all.

The Three Musketeers

37.5 And they saw, by the red flashes of the
lightning against the violet fog which the
wind stamped upon the backward sky... they
saw pass gravely, at six paces behind the
governor, a man clothed in black, and
masked by a visor of polished steel, soldered
to a helmet of the same nature, which
altogether enveloped the whole of his head.

The Man in the Iron Mask

38.1 D'Artangnan endeavoured to raise himself up ... then, clasping in his nerveless hand the baton ornamented with its fleur-de-lis, he cast down upon it his eyes which had no longer the power of looking upwards towards heaven, and fell back, murmuring those strange words, which appeared to the soldiers cabalistic words—words which had formerly represented so many things upon earth, and which none but the dying man longer comprehended.

'Athos—Porthos, farewell till we meet again! Aramis, adieu forever!'

Of the four valiant men whose history we have related, there now no longer remained but one single body; God had resumed the souls.

Ib.

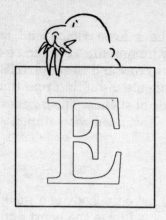

Thomas Alva Edison 1847-1931

39.1 Genius is one percent inspiration and ninety-nine percent perspiration.

Newspaper interview, 1931

George Eliot (Mary Ann Cross) 1819-1880

39.2 'O mother,' said Maggie, 'I don't *want* to do my patchwork
'It's foolish work,' said Maggie, with a toss of her hair, 'tearing things to pieces to sew them together again.'

The Mill on the Floss

39.3 A woman's no business wi' being so clever; it'll turn to trouble, I doubt.

Ib.

40.1 If we had a keen vision and feeling of all ordinary human life, it would be like hearing the grass grow and the squirrel's heart beat, and we should die of that roar that lies on the other side of silence. The quickest of us walk about well wadded with stupidity.

Middlemarch

Elizabeth I 1533-1603

40.2 I know I have the body of a weak and feeble woman, but I have the heart and stomach of a king, and of a king of England too.

Speech at Tilbury at the approach of the Spanish Armada, 1588.

Ralph Waldo Emerson 1803-1882

40.3 The louder he talked of his honour, the faster we counted the spoons.

Conduct of Life

40.4 If a man write a better book, preach a better sermon, or make a better mouse-trap than his neighbour, tho' he build his house in the woods, the world will make a beaten path to his door.

Attrib.

Robert Emmet 1778-1803

41.1 Let no man write my epitaph; for as no man who knows my motives dare now vindicate them, let not prejudice or ignorance asperse them.

> Speech from the dock, 20 Sept 1903

41.2 Let my memory be left in oblivion, my tomb remain uninscribed, until other times and other men can do justice to my character. When my country takes her place among the nations of the earth, *then* and *not till then*, let my epitaph be written.

> *Ib.*

Eugene Field 1850-1895

42.1 The little toy dog is covered with dust,
    But sturdy and staunch he stands;
  And the little toy soldier is red with rust,
    And the musket moulds in his hands.
  Time was when the little toy dog was new,
    And the soldier was passing fair;
  And that was the time when our Little Boy
    Blue
    Kissed them and put them there.

'Little Boy Blue'

42.2 Wynken, Blynken and Nod one night
  Sailed off in a wooden shoe—
  Sailed on a river of crystal light,
  Into a sea of dew.

'Wynken, Blynken and Nod'

James Elroy Flecker 1884-1915

43.1 A ship, an isle, a sickle moon—
With few but with how splendid stars.

'A Ship, an Isle, a Sickle Moon'

43.2 I have seen old ships sail like swans asleep.

'The Old Ships'

Henry Ford 1863-1947

43.3 History is more or less bunk.

Chicago Tribune 25 May 1916

Lena Guilbert Ford

43.4 Keep the home fires burning, while your
hearts are yearning,
Though your lads are far away they dream
of home;
There's a silver lining through the dark
clouds shining:
Turn the dark cloud inside out till the boys
come home.

'Keep the Home Fires Burning.'

Benjamin Franklin 1706-1790

43.5 A little neglect may breed mischief ... for
want of a nail, the shoe was lost; for want of a
shoe the horse was lost; for want of a horse
the rider was lost

Poor Richard's Almanac

44.1 Early to bed, and early to rise,
Makes a man healthy, wealthy and wise.

Ib.

44.2 We must indeed all hang together, or, most
assuredly, we shall all hang separately.

Remark at the signing of
the Declaration of Independence, 1776.

44.3 Here Skugg lies snug,
As a bug in a rug.

'Epitaph for Georgina Shipley's pet squirrel.'

44.4 The body of
Benjamin Franklin, printer,
(Like the cover of an old book,
Its contents worn out,
And stript of its lettering and gilding)
Lies here food for worms!
Yet the work itself shall not be lost.
For it will, as he believed, appear once more
In a new
And more beautiful edition,
Corrected and amended
By its Author!

'Epitaph for himself.'

Sir Gregory Gander (George Ellis) 1745-1815

45.1 Snowy, Flowy, Blowy,
Showery, Flowery, Bowery,
Hoppy, Croppy, Droppy,
Breezy, Sneezy, Freezy.

'The Twelve Months'

William Schwenck Gilbert 1836-1911

45.2 Oh, I am a cook and a captain bold,
And the mate of the *Nancy* brig,
And a bo'sun tight, and a midshipmite,
And the crew of the captain's gig.

'The Yarn of the Nancy Bell'

45.3 He led his regiment from behind—
He found it less exciting.

The Gondoliers

46.1   The House of Peers, throughout the war,
Did nothing in particular,
And did it very well.

Iolanthe

46.2   A wandering minstrel I—
A thing of shreds and patches.

The Mikado

46.3   On a tree by a river a little tom-tit
Sang 'Willow, titwillow, titwillow.

Ib.

46.4   I never use a big, big D.

HMS Pinafore

46.5   When constabulary duty's to be done
The policeman's lot is not a happy one.

The Pirates of Penzance

46.6   She may very well pass for forty-three
In the dusk with the light behind her!

Trial by Jury

Oliver Goldsmith 1730-1774
46.7   The loud laugh that spoke the vacant mind.

The Deserted Village

47.1 Truth from his lips prevailed with double
  sway,
 And fools who came to scoff remained to
  pray.

          Ib. 'The Village Parson'

47.2 Amazed the gazing rustics rang'd around,
 And still they gaz'd and still the wonder
  grew,
 That one small head could carry all he
  knew.

        Ib. 'The Village Schoolmaster'

47.3 The man recover'd of the bite
 The dog it was that died.

        'Elegy on the Death of a Mad Dog'

47.4 On stage he was natural, simple, affecting;
 'Twas only that when he was off he was
  acting.

           On Garrick

47.5 This is Liberty-Hall, gentlemen.

         She Stoops to Conquer

George Gordon, Lord Byron 1788-1824

47.6 So, we'll go no more a roving
  So late into the night,
 Though the heart be still as loving
  And the moon be still as bright.

       'So We'll Go No More a-Roving'

Richard Grafton d.1572

48.1 Thirty days hath November,
April, June, and September,
February hath twenty-eight alone
And all the rest have thirty-one.

Abridgement of the Chronicles of England

Harry Graham 1874-1936

48.2 Billy in one of his nice new sashes,
Fell in the fire and was burned to ashes;
Now, although the room grows chilly,
I haven't the heart to poke poor Billy.

Ruthless Rhymes. 'Tender-Heartedness'

48.3 Oe'r the rugged mountain's brow
Clara threw the twins she nursed,
And remarked, 'I wonder now
Which will reach the bottom first?'

Ib. 'Calculating Clara'

48.4 'There's been an accident!' they said,
'Your servant's cut in half; he's dead!'
'Indeed!' said Mr Jones, 'and please
Send me the half that's got my keys.'

Ib. 'Mr Jones'

Kenneth Grahame 1859-1932

49.1 There is nothing—absolutely nothing—half
so much worth doing as simply messing
about in boats.

The Wind in theWillows

John Woodcock Gravens 1795-1886

49.2 D'ye ken John Peel with his coat so gray?
D'ye ken John Peel at the break of day?
D'ye ken John Peel when he's far far away
With his hounds and his horn in the
morning?

'D'ye ken John Peel'

Arthur Perceval Graves 1846-1931

49.3 Of priests we can offer a charming variety,
Far renowned for larnin' and piety;
Still, I'd advance ye widout impropriety,
Father O'Flynn as the flower of them all.

'Father O'Flynn'

Thomas Gray 1716-1771

49.4 The curfew tolls the knell of parting day,
The lowing herd winds slowly o'er the lea,
The ploughman homewards plods his weary
way
And leaves the world to darkness and to
me.

'Elegy Written in a Country Churchyard.'

50.1 The paths of glory lead but to the grave.

Ib.

50.2 Full many a flower is born to blush,
And waste its sweetness on the desert air.

Ib.

50.3 ... where ignorance is bliss,
'Tis folly to be wise.

'Ode on a Distant Prospect of Eton College.'

Horace Greeley 1811-1872

50.4 Go west, young man, and grow up with the
country.

Hints towards Reform

George & Weedon Grossmith 1847-1912 and 1854-1919

50.5 I left the room with silent dignity, but caught
my foot in the mat.

The Diary of a Nobody

Dorothy Gurney 1858-1932

50.6 The kiss of the sun for pardon,
The song of the birds for mirth,
One is nearer God's Heart in a garden
Than anywhere else on earth.

'God's Garden'

H Rider Haggard 1856-1923

51.1 She-who-must-be-obeyed

She

Sarah Josepha Hale 1788-1879

51.2 Mary had a little lamb,
         Its fleece was white as snow,
      And everywhere that Mary went
         The lamb was sure to go.

Poems for Our Children; 'Mary's Little Lamb'

Charles Graham Halpine 1829-1868

51.3 You'll see O'Ryan any night
      Amid the constellations.

Irish Astronomy

Sir John Harington 1561-1919

52.1 Treason doth never prosper: what's the
      reason?
      For if it prosper, none dare call it treason.

Epigrams

Charles K Harris 1865-1930

52.2 Many a heart is aching, if you could read
      them all
      Many the hopes that have vanished, after
      the ball.

'After the Ball'

Joel Chandler Harris 1848-1908

52.3 Hit look lak sparrer-grass, hit feel lak spar-
      rer-grass, hit tas'e lak sparrer-grass, en I
      bless ef 'taint sparrer-grass.

'Asparagus' *Uncle Remus*

52.4 Tar-baby ain't sayin' nuthin', en Brer Fox,
      he lay low.

Ib.

'Ian Hay' John Hay Beith 1876-1952

52.5 Funny peculiar, or funny ha-ha?

The Housemaster

William Hazlitt 1778-1830

52.6 One of the pleasantest things in the world is
      going a journey; but I like to go by myself.

On Going a Journey.

53.1 Give me the clear blue sky above my head,
and the green turf beneath my feet, a
winding road before me, and a three hours
march to dinner.

Ib.

Felicia Dorothea Hemans 1793-1835

53.2 The boy stood on the burning deck
  Whence all but he had fled.

'Casabianca'

William Ernest Henley 1849-1903

53.3 In the fell clutch of circumstance,
I have not winced nor cried aloud;
Under the bludgeoning of chance
My head is bloody but unbowed.

'Invictus'

53.4 It matters not how strait the gate,
How charged with punishments the scroll,
I am the master of my fate:
I am the captain of my soul.

Ib.

Robert Herrick 1591-1674

53.5 Her eyes the glow-worm lend thee,
The shooting-stars attend thee;
And the elves also,
Whose little eyes glow
Like the sparks of fire, befriend thee.

'The Night-Piece, to Julia'

54.1 Gather ye rosebuds while ye may,
　　Old Time is still a-flying;
　　And this same flower that smiles today,
　　To-morrow will be dying.

'To Virgins, To make Much of Time'

54.2 In the morning when ye rise
　　Wash your hands, and cleanse your eyes.
　　Next be sure ye have a care,
　　To disperse the water farre.
　　For as farre as that doth light,
　　So farre keeps the evill Spright.

'Charme'

Brewster Higley fl 1873

54.3 Home, home on the range,
　　　Where the deer and the antelope play
　　Where seldom is heard a discouraging word,
　　　And the skies are not cloudy all day.

'Home on the Range'

Katherine Tynan Hinkson 1861-1931

54.4 All in the April evening,
　　April airs were abroad,
　　I saw the sheep with their lambs
　　And thought on the Lamb of God.

'Sheep and Lambs'

Edward Wallis Hoch 1849-1925

55.1 There is so much good in the worst of us,
And so much bad in the best of us,
That it hardly becomes any of us
To talk about the rest of us.

'Good and Bad'

Heinrich Hoffman 1809-1894

55.2 Augustus was a chubby lad;
Fat ruddy cheeks Augustus had.
And everbody saw with joy
The plump and hearty, healthy boy.
He ate and drank as he was told,
But one day, one cold winter's day,
He screamed out 'Take the soup away!
O take the nasty soup away!
I won't have any soup today.

'The Story of Augustus who would Not have any Soup'
(Trans. from the German)

55.3 Look at him, now the fourth day's come!
He scarcely weighs a sugar-plum;
He's like a little bit of thread,
And, on the fifth day, he was—dead!

Ib.

56.1　As he trudged along to school,
　　　It was always Johnny's rule
　　　To be looking at the sky
　　　And the clouds that floated by;
　　　But what just before him lay
　　　Johnny never thought about;
　　　So that everyone cried out
　　　'Look at little Johnny there,
　　　Little Johnny Head-in-Air!'

'The Story of Johnny Head-in-Air'

James Hogg 1770-1835

56.2　Where the pools are bright and deep,
　　　Where the gray trout lies asleep,
　　　Up the river and o'er the lea.
　　　That's the way for Billy and me.

'A Boy's Song'

Thomas Hood 1799-1845

56.3　I remember, I remember,
　　　The house where I was born,
　　　The little window where the sun
　　　Came peeping in at morn;
　　　He never came a wink too soon,
　　　Nor brought too long a day,
　　　But now, I often wish the night
　　　Had borne my breath away!

'I Remember'

57.1 No warmth, no cheerfulness, no healthful
    ease,
No comfortable feel in any member—
No shade, no shine, no butterflies, no bees,
No fruits, no flowers, no leaves, no birds,
November!

                      'No!'

A E Housman 1859-1936

57.2 I, a stranger and afraid,
In a world I never made.

                 Last Poems xii

57.3 Loveliest of trees, the cherry now
Is hung with bloom along the bough.

               A Shropshire Lad ii

57.4 With rue my heart is laden
    For golden friends I had
For many a rose-lipt maiden
    And many a lightfoot lad.

                   Ib. liv

Julia Ward Howe 1819-1910

57.5 Mine eyes have seen the glory of the coming
    of the Lord;
He is trampling out the vintage where the
    grapes of wrath are stored;
He has loosed the fatal lightning of his
    terrible swift sword:
His truth is marching on.

          'Battle Hymn of the Republic'

Mary Howitt 1799-1888

58.1 'Will you walk into my parlour?' said the
Spider to the Fly,
''Tis the prettiest little parlour that ever
you did spy;
The way into my parlour is up a winding
stair,
And I have many curious things to show
when you are there.'
'Oh no, no,' said the little Fly, 'to ask me is
in vain,
For who goes up your winding stair can
ne'er come down again.'

'The Spider and the Fly'

Edmond Hoyle 1672-1769

58.2 When in doubt, win the trick.

Whist

Thomas Hughes 1822-1896

58.3 Life isn't all beer and skittles.

Tom Brown's Schooldays

58.4 He never wants anything but what's right
and fair; only when you come to settle what's
right and fair it's everything that he wants
and nothing that you want. And that's his
idea of a compromise.

Ib.

58.5 It's more than a game. It's an institution.
(Cricket)

Ib.

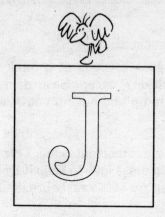

Thomas Jefferson 1743-1826

59.1 We hold these truths to be self-evident, that
all men are created equal, that they are
endowed by their Creator with certain
unalienable Rights, that among these are
Life, Liberty and the Pursuit of Happiness.

The Declaration of Independence (Final Form) 4 July 1776.

Jerome K Jerome 1859-1927

59.2 Cholera I had, with severe complications;
and diphtheria I seemed to have been born
with. I plodded conscientiously through the
twenty-six letters, and the only malady I
could conclude I had not got was housemaid's
knee.

Three Men in a Boat

60.1 George goes to sleep at a bank from ten to four each day, except Saturdays, when they wake him up and put him outside at two.

Ib.

60.2 I like work: it fascinates me. I can sit and look at if for hours. I love to keep it by me; the idea of getting rid of it nearly breaks my heart.

Ib.

Dr Samuel Johnson (Conferred by Trinity College, Dublin) 1709-1784

60.3 The Irish are a fair people; they never speak well of one another.

Boswell, *Life of Johnson*, 1775

60.4 Boswell: Is not the Giant's Causeway worth seeing?
Johnson: Worth seeing? yes; but not worth going to see.

Ib. 12 October 1779

James (Augustine) Joyce 1882-1941

60.5 Stephen Daedalus is my name
Ireland is my nation.
Clongowes is my dwellingplace
And heaven my expectation.

A Portrait of the Artist as a Young Man

61.1 Do you know what Ireland is? asked Stephen
with cold violence.
Ireland is the old sow that eats her farrow.

Ib.

61.2 I will not serve that in which I no longer
believe,
whether it call itself my home my father, or
my church:
and I will try to express myself in some mode
of life or art
as freely as I can and as wholly as I can, using
for my defence
the only arms I allow myself to use—silence,
exile, and cunning.

Ib.

Robert Dwyer Joyce 1830-1883

61.3 We are the boys of Wexford
Who fought with heart and hand
To break in twain the galling chain
And free our native land.

'The Boys of Wexford'

Patrick Kavanagh 1906-1967

62.1 My father played the melodeon,
      My mother milked the cows,
      And I had a prayer like a white rose pinned
      On the Virgin Mary's blouse.

                                    'A Christmas Childhood'

Peadar Kearney 1883-1942

62.2 Soldiers are we, whose lives are pledged to
      Ireland.

                                    'A Soldier's Song'

John Keats 1795-1821

63.1 There was a naughty boy
        And a naughty boy was he
      He ran away to Scotland
        The people for to see.

'A Song about Myself'

Thomas Kettle 1880-1916

63.2 Know that we fools, now with the foolish
            dead,
      Died not for the flag, nor King, nor
            Emperor,
      But for a dream, born in a herdsman's shed,
      And for the secret Scripture of the poor.

'To My Daughter Betty, the Gift of God'

Francis Scott Key 1779-1843

63.3 'Tis the star-spangled banner; O long may it
      wave
      O'er the land of the free, and the home of the
      brave.'

'The Star-Spangled Banner'

Benjamin Franklin King 1857-1894

63.4 Nothing to do but work
      Nothing to eat but food,
      Nothing to wear but clothes
      To keep from going nude.

'The Pessimist'

64.1 Nothing to breathe but air,
    Quick as a flash 'tis gone;
    Nowhere to fall but off,
    Nowhere to stand but on!

Ib.

Charles Kingsley 1819-1875

64.2 When all the world is young, lad,
    And all the trees are green;
    And every goose a swan, lad,
    And every lass a queen;
    Then hey for boot and horse, lad,
    And round the world away;
    Young blood must have its course, lad,
    And every dog his day.

'Young and Old'

Rudyard Kipling 1865-1936

64.3 Oh, East is East, and West is West, and never
the twain shall meet.

'The Ballad of East and West'

64.4 When the Himalayan peasant meets the
    he-bear in his pride,
    He shouts to scare the monster, who often
    turns aside.
    But the she-bear thus accosted rends the
    peasant tooth and nail
    For the female of the species is more deadly
    than the male.

'The Female of the Species'

65.1 The uniform he wore
      Was nothin' much before,
      An' rather less that 'arf o' that behind.

'Gunga Din'

65.2 If you can fill the unforgiving minute
      With sixty seconds' worth of distance run
      Yours is the Earth and everything that's in it,
      And—what is more—you'll be a Man, my son!

'If'

65.3 Ship me somewhere east of Suez, where the
      best is like the worst,
      Where there aren't no Ten Commandments,
      an' a man can raise a thirst.

'Mandalay'

Frederick Langbridge 1849-1923

66.1 Two men look out through the same bars:
One sees mud, and one the stars.

'A Cluster of Quiet Thoughts'

Bishop Hugh Latimer 1485-1555

66.2 Be of good comfort, Master Ridley, and play
the man. We shall this day light such a
candle by God's grace in England, as (I trust)
shall never he put out.

Said when he and Ridley were about to be
burned at the stake

Stephen Leacock 1869-1944

67.1 The landlady of a boarding-house is a parallelogram—that is an oblong angular figure, which cannot be described, but which is equal to anything.

'Boarding-House Geometry'

67.2 He flung himself from the room, flung himself upon his horse and rode madly off in all directions.

'Gertrude the Governess'

Edward Lear 1812-1888

67.3 There was an Old Man with a beard,
Who said, 'It's just as I feared!—
Two Owls and a Hen
Four Larks and a Wren,
Have all built their nests in my beard!'

67.4 The Owl and the Pussy-Cat went to sea
In a beautiful pea-green boat.

'The Owl and the Pussy-Cat'

67.5 They dined on mince and slices of quince,
Which they ate with a runcible spoon;
And hand in hand, on the edge of the sand,
They danced by the light of the moon.

Ib.

68.1 'It's a fact the whole world knows,
That Pobbles are happier without their toes.

'The Pobble Who Has No Toes'

Winifred M Letts 1882-1950

68.2 A soft day, thank God!
A wind from the south
With a honeyed mouth.

'A Soft Day'

Abraham Lincoln 1809-1865

68.3 ... that we here highly resolve that the dead shall not have died in vain, that this nation, under God, shall have a new birth of freedom; and that government of the people, by the people, and for the people shall not perish from the earth.

Address at Dedication of National Cemetery at Gettysburg,
19 November 1863

68.4 With malice towards none; with charity for all; with firmness in the right, as God gives us to see the right, let us strive on to finish the work we are in.

Speech, 4 March 1864

68.5 You can fool all the people some of the time, and some of the people all of the time but you cannot fool all the people all the time.

Attrib.

John Locke 1847-1889

69.1 O Ireland isn't it grand you look—
      Like a bride in her rich adornin'?
      And with all the pent-up love of my heart
      I bid you the top of the mornin'!

'The Exile's Return'

Henry Wadsworth Longfellow 1807-1882

69.2 Lives of great men all remind us
          We can make our lives sublime,
      And departing leave behind us
          Footprints on the sands of time.

'The Reaper and the Flowers'

69.3 Under a spreading chestnut tree
          The village smithy stands;
      The smith, a mighty man is he,
          With large and sinewy hands;
      And the muscle of his brawny arms
          Are strong as iron bands.

'The Village Blacksmith'

69.4 Listen, my children, and you shall hear
      Of the midnight ride of Paul Revere.

'Paul Revere's Ride'

70.1 There was a little girl
Who had a little curl
Right in the middle of her forehead.
When she was good
She was very, very good,
But when she was bad she was horrid.

'There Was a Little Girl'

Richard Lovelace 1618-1658

70.2 Stone walls do not a prison make
Nor iron bars a cage.

'To Lucasta, Going Beyond the Seas'

70.3 I could not love thee (Dear) so much,
Lov'd I not honour more.

'To Lucasta, Going to the Wars'

St. Ignatius Loyola 1491-1556

70.4 To give and not to count the cost;
To fight and not to heed the wounds;
To toil and not to seek for rest;
To labour and not ask for any reward
Save that of knowing that we do Thy will.

'Prayer for Generosity'

Henry Francis Lyte 1793-1847

70.5 Swift to the close ebbs out life's little day;
Earth's joy's grow dim, its glories pass away;
Change and decay in all around I see;
O Thou, who changest not, abide with me.

'Abide With Me'

Thomas Babington Lord Macauley 1800-1859

71.1 Every schoolboy knows who imprisoned Montezuma, and who strangled Atahualpa.

Historical Essays 'Lord Clive'

71.2 The Puritan hated bear-baiting, not because it gave pain to the bear, but because it gave pleasure to the spectators.

History of England

71.3 We know so spectacle so ridiculous as the British public in one of its periodical fits of morality

Literary Essays 'Moore's Life of Byron'

George MacDonald 1824-1905

72.1 Where did you come from, baby dear?
Out of the everywhere into here.

'At the Back of the North Wind'

72.2 Where did you get your eyes so blue?
Out of the sky as I came through.

Ib.

Marshal McMahon 1808-1893

72.3 J'y suis, j'y reste.
(Here I am and here I stay).

Attrib. at taking of Malakoff, 1855

Francis Sylvester Mahony 1804-1866

72.4 'Tis the bells of Shandon,
That sound so grand on
The pleasant waters
Of the River Lee.

'The Bells of Shandon'

Queen Marie Antoinette 1755-1793

72.5 Qu'ils mangent de la brioche.
(Let them eat cake).

Attrib. on being told that the people could not afford bread

W R Mandale 19th Century

73.1 Up and down the City Road
In and out the Eagle
That's the way the money goes—
Pop goes the weasel!

'Pop goes the Weasel'

Christopher Marlowe 1564-1593

73.2 Was this the face that launch'd a thousand
ships
And burnt the topless towers of Ilium?

Doctor Faustus

Rev William Frederick Marshall 1882-1959

73.3 I'm livin' in Drumlister
An I'm gettin' very oul'
I have to wear an Indian bag
To save me from the coul'
The deil a man in this townlan'
Wos claner raired nor me,
But I'm livin' in Drumlister
In clabber to the knee.

'Me an' Me Da'

Andrew Marvell 1620-1687

73.4 The grave's a fine and private place,
But none I think do there embrace.

'To His Coy Mistress'

John Masefield 1878-1967

74.1 I must go down to the seas again, to the
lonely sea and the sky,
And all I ask is a tall ship and a star to steer
her by.

'Sea Fever'

Charlotte Mew 1869-1928

74.2 Why did they bring me here to make me
Not quite bad and not quite good,
Why unless They're wicked, do They want, in
spite to take me
Back to their wet, wild wood?

'The Changeling'

William Miller 1810-1872

74.3 Wee Willie Winkie rins through the town,
Up stairs and doon stairs in his nicht gown,
Tirling at the window, crying at the lock,
'Are the weans in their bed, for it's now ten
o'clock?'

'Willie Winkie'

A A Milne 1882-1956

74.4 They're changing guard at Buckingham
Palace—
Christopher Robin went down with Alice.
Alice is marrying one of the guard.
'A soldier's life is terrible hard,'
Says Alice

'Buckingham Palace'

75.1 Little Boy kneels at the foot of the bed,
Droops on his little hands little gold head.
Hush! Hush! Whisper who dares!
Christopher Robin is saying his prayers.

'Vespers'

James Lynam Molloy 1837-1909

75.2 As I'm sitting all alone in the gloaming,
The shadows of the past draw near,
And I see the loving faces round me
That used to glad the old stone pier.

'Bantry Bay'

75.3 Time goes by and the happy years are dead,
And one by one the merry hearts are fled;
Silent now is the wild and lonely glen
Where the bright glad laugh will echo ne'er
    again.

'The Kerry Dance'

Percy Montrose fl 1880

75.4 In a cavern, in a canyon
    Excavating for a mine,
Dwelt a miner, forty-niner,
    And his daughter, Clementine.

'Clementine'

75.5 Oh my darling, oh my darling,
Oh my darling Clementine;
You are lost and gone forever,
Oh my darling Clementine

Ib.

Clement Clarke Moore 1779-1863

76.1 'Twas the night before Christmas, when all
   through the house
  Not a creature was stirring, not even a
   mouse;
  The stockings were hung by the chimney
   with care,
  In hopes that St Nicholas soon would be
   there.

           'The Night before Christmas'

76.2 'Now, *Dasher!* now, *Dancer!* now, *Prancer*
  and *Vixen!*
  On, *Comet!* on, *Cupid!* on, *Donder* and
  Blitzen!'

                Ib.

Thomas Moore 1779-1852

76.3 Erin, the tear and the smile in thine eyes,
  Blend like the rainbow that hangs in thy
   skies!

              'Erin, the Tear'

76.4 The harp that once through Tara's halls
   The soul of music shed,
  Now hangs as mute on Tara's walls
   As if that soul were fled.

            'The Harp that Once'

77.1 'Tis the last rose of summer
    Left blooming alone;
All her lovely companions
    Are faded and gone

             'The Last Rose of Summer'

77.2 The Minstrel Boy to the war is gone
    In the ranks of death you'll find him;
His father's sword he has girded on
    And his wild harp slung behind him.

             'The Minstrel Boy'

77.3 Oft in the stilly night
Ere Slumber's chain hath bound me,
Fond Memory brings the light
Of other days around me.

             'Oft in The Stilly Night'

Thomas Osbert Mordaunt 1730-1809

77.4 Sound, sound the clarion, fill the fife,
    Throughout the sensual world proclaim,
One crowded hour of glorious life
    Is worth an age without a name.

             'Sound, Sound the Clarion'

William Mulchineck 1820-1864

77.5 Tho' lovely and fair as the rose of the summer
    Yet 'twas not her beauty alone that won me,
Oh, no 'twas the truth in her eyes ever
      beaming
That made me love Mary, the Rose of Tralee.

             'The Rose of Tralee'

Carolina Baroness Nairne 1766-1845

78.1 Charlie is my darling, my darling,
        my darling,
        Charlie is my darling, the young Chevalier.

'Charlie is My Darling'

Napoleon Bonaparte 1769-1821

78.2 Every French soldier carries in his cartridge-
        pouch the baton of a marshal of France.

Attrib.

78.3 From the sublime to the ridiculous there is
        only one step.

After the retreat from Moscow.

79.1 An army marches on its stomach

Attrib.

Ogden Nash 1902-1971

79.2 The one-l lama,
He's a priest.
The two-l llama,
He's a beast.
And I will bet
A silk pyjama
There isn't any
Three-l lllama.

Thomas Nashe 1567-1601

79.3 Brightness falls from the air;
Queens have died young and fair;
Dust hath closed Helen's eye.

'In Time of Pestilence'

John Mason Neale 1818-1866

79.4 Good King Wenceslas look'd out,
On the Feast of Stephen
When the snow lay round about
Deep and crisp and even.

'Good King Wenceslas'

Horatio Nelson 1758-1805

79.5 England expects every man to do his duty.

Signal at Trafalgar, 9 October 1805

Sir Henry John Newbolt 1862-1938

80.1 There's a breathless hush in the Close to-
    night—
  Ten to make and the match to win—
    A bumping pitch and a blinding light
  An hour to play and the last man in.

'Vitai Lampada'

80.2 The voice of the schoolboy rallies the ranks:
  'Play up! play up! and play the game!'

Ib.

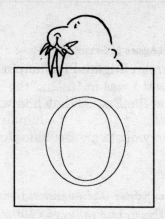

Sean O'Casey 1882-1964

81.1 The last o' the Mohicans ... The blinds is
down, Joxer, the blinds is down.

Juno and the Paycock

81.2 I'm tellin' you ... Joxer ... th' whole world's ...
in a terr...ible state o' ... chassis.

Ib.

Daniel O'Connell 1775-1847

81.3 Not for all the universe contains would I, in
the struggle for what I conceive my country's
cause, consent to the effusion of a single drop
of human blood, except my own.

Speech, 28 February 1843

Moira O'Neill (Agnes M Skrine) c.1870—?

82.1 Over here in England I'm helpin' wi' the hay,
An' I wisht I was in Ireland the livelong day;
Weary on the English hay and sorra take the
   wheat!
Och, Corrymeala an' the blue sky over it!

'Corrymeala'

Arthur William Edgar O'Shaughnessy 1844-1881

82.2 We are the music makers,
We are the dreamers of dreams.

'We are the Music Makers'

George Orwell 1903-1950

82.3 Four legs good, two legs bad.

Animal Farm

82.4 All animals are equal, but some animals are
more equal than others.

Ib.

82.5 Big Brother is watching you

1984

Wilfred Owen 1893-1918

83.1 If you could hear, at every jolt, the blood
Come gargling from the froth-corrupted
lungs,
Bitter as the cud
Of vile, incurable sores on innocent
tongues—
My friend, you would not tell with such high
zest
To children ardent for some desperate glory,
The old lie: Dulce et decorum est
Pro patria mori.

'Dulce et Decorum Est'

Viscount Palmerston 1784-1865

84.1 Die, my dear Doctor, that's the last thing I shall do!

Attrib. last words

Charles Stewart Parnell 1846-1891

84.2 When a man takes a farm from which another has been evicted, you must show him in the streets of the town, you must show him in the fair and in the market-place, and even in the house of worship, by leaving him severely alone, by putting him into moral Coventry, by isolating him from his kind as if he was a leper of old ...

Speech at Ennis, 18 September 1880.

85.1 ... no man has the right to fix the boundary of the march of a nation. No man has the right to say to his country, 'Thus far shalt thou go and no further,' and we have never attempted to fix the *ne plus ultra* to the progress of Ireland's nationhood and we never shall.

Speech at Cork, 21 January 1885

Andrew Paterson 1864-1941

85.2 Once a jolly swagman camped by a billy-
bong,
Under the shade of a kulibar tree,
And he sang as he sat and waited for his billy-
boil,
'You'll come a-waltzing, Matilda, with me.'

'Waltzing Matilda'

Pope John Paul II (Karol Wojtyla)

85.3 Young people of Ireland, I love you;
Young people of Ireland, I bless you.

Address at Ballybrit Racecourse, Galway,
30 September 1979

James Payn 1830-1898

85.4 I never had a piece of toast
Particularly long and wide,
But fell upon the sanded floor.
And always on the buttered side.

'Chambers's Journal' (Parody of Tom Moore's 'Lala Rookh')

John Howard Payne 1791-1852

86.1 Mid pleasures and palaces though we may
roam,
Be it ever so humble, there's no place like
home.

Clari, the Maid of Milan. 'Home Sweet Home'

Thomas Love Peacock 1785-1866

86.2 A book that furnishes no quotations is ... no
book—it is a plaything.

'Crotchet Castle'

86.3 The mountain sheep are sweeter,
But the valley sheep are fatter;
We therefore deemed it meeter
To carry off the latter.

'The War-Song of Dinas Vawr'

Padraic Pearse 1879-1916

86.4 The beauty of the world hath made me sad,
This beauty that will pass;

'The Wayfarer'

86.5 ... The fools, the fools, the fools!— they have
left us our Fenian dead and while Ireland
holds these graves, Ireland unfree shall
never be at peace.

Oration at the graveside of O'Donovan Rossa, 1915

Samuel Pepys 1633-1703

87.1 And so to bed.

Diary 20 April 1660

87.2 I went to Charing Cross, to see Major-General Harrison hanged, drawn, and quartered, which was done there, he looking as cheerful as any man could in that condition.

Ib. 13 October 1660

William Pitt, Earl of Chatham 1708-1778

87.3 The atrocious crime of being a young man ... I shall neither attempt to palliate nor deny.

Speech in the House of Commons 27 January 1741.

Edgar Allan Poe 1809-1849

87.4 Thy Naiad airs have brought me home
To the glory that was Greece
And the grandeur that was Rome.

'To Helen'

Alexander Pope 1688-1744

87.5 What beck'ning ghost, along the moonlight shade
Invites my steps, and points to yonder glade.

'Elegy to the Memory of an Unfortunate Lady'

88.1 True wit is nature to advantage dressed,
What oft was thought, but ne'er so well
expressed.

'Essay on Criticism'

88.2 'Tis with our judgments as our watches,
none
Go just alike, yet each believes his own.

Ib.

88.3 True ease in writing comes from art, not
chance.

Ib.

88.4 Where'er you find 'the cooling western
breeze'
In the next line, it 'whispers through the
trees':
If crystal streams 'with pleasing murmurs
creep'
The reader's threatened, not in vain, with
'sleep.'

Ib.

Ezra Pound 1885-1972 *

88.5 Winter is icummen in,
Lhude sing Goddamn.
Raineth drop and staineth slop,
And how the wind doth ramm!
Sing Goddamn.

'Ancient Music'

* See 9.2

The Book of Common Prayer 1553

89.1 We have left undone those things which we
      ought to have done;
      And we have done those things which we
      ought not to have done;

General Confession

89.2 Read, mark, learn and inwardly digest.

Collect, 2nd Sunday in Advent

89.3 To have and to hold from this day forward, for
      better for worse, for richer for poorer in
      sickness and in health, to love and to cherish,
      till death us to part.

Solemnization of Matrimony

89.4 Man that is born of a woman hath but a short
      time to live and is full of misery.

The Burial of the Dead

89.5 In the midst of life we are in death.

Ib.

89.6 We therefore commit his body to the ground;
      earth to earth, ashes to ashes, dust to dust; in
      sure and certain hope of the Resurrection to
      eternal life.

Ib.

Israel Putnam 1718-1790

90.1 Men, you are all marksmen—don't one of you
fire until you see the whites of their eyes.

> At Bunker Hill, the first battle of the American
> War of Independence, 1775.

Sir Walter A Raleigh 1861-1922

91.1　I wish I loved the Human Race;
　　　I wish I loved its silly face;
　　　I wish I liked the way it walks;
　　　I wish I liked the way it talks.
　　　And when I'm introduced to one
　　　I wish I thought What Jolly Fun!

'Wishes of an Elderly Man'

William Brightly Rands 1823-1882

91.2　I wish I lived in a caravan,
　　　With a horse to drive, like a pedlar-man!
　　　Where he comes from nobody knows,
　　　Or where he goes to, but on he goes!

'The Pedlar's Caravan'

Grantland Rice 1880-1954

92.1 For when the One Great Scorer comes
To write against your name,
He marks—not that you won or lost—
But how you played the game.

'Alumnus Football'

Cardinal Richelieu 1585-1642

92.2 If you give you me six lines written by the most honest man, I will find something in them to hang him.

Attrib.

President Franklin D. Roosevelt 1882-1945

92.3 I pledge you—I pledge myself—to a new deal for the American people.

Chicago Convention—1932

92.4 Let me assert my firm belief that the only thing we have to fear is fear itself.

First Inaugural Address 1933.

President Theodore Roosevelt 1858-1919

92.5 There is a homely adage which runs 'Speak softly and carry a big stick.'

Minnesota State Fair, 2 September 1901

Christina Rossetti 1830-1894

93.1 Who has seen the wind?
Neither I nor you:
But when the leaves hang trembling,
The wind is passing thro'.

'Who Has Seen The Wind?'

93.2 Who has seen the wind?
Neither you nor I:
But when the trees bow down their heads,
The wind is passing by.

Ib.

Patrick Sarsfield, Earl of Lucan (d. 1693)

94.1 Sarsfield is the watchword—Sarsfield is the
man

At Ballyneety, 11 August 1690

94.2 Change kings and we will fight it over again
with you.

After Limerick, Attrib.

94.3 Would to God this was shed for Ireland.

Attrib. last words fighting for France at Landen.

Sir Walter Scott 1771-1832

94.4 Breathes there a man, with soul so dead,
Who never to himself hath said,
This is my own, my native land.

'The Lay of the Last Minstrel'

95.1 Come fill up my cup, come fill up my can
Come saddle the horses and call up the
    men,
Come open your gates, and let me gae free,
For its's up with the bonnets of Bonny
    Dundee!

'Bonny Dundee'

95.2 There was racing and chasing on Cannobie
    Lea,
But the lost bride of Netherby ne'er did they
    see.
So daring in love, and so dauntless in war,
Have ye e'er heard of gallant like young
    Lochinvar.

'Young Lochinvar'

W C Sellar 1898-1951 & **R J Yeatman** 1898-1968

95.3 The Roman Conquest was, however, a Good
Thing.

1066, And All That

95.4 The memorable epitaph: 'Honi soi qui mal y
pense'
('Honey, your silk stocking's hanging down.')

Ib.

95.5 Finding however, that he was not
particularly memorable, he very patriot-
ically abdicated in favour of Henry IV,
part II.

Ib.

96.1 A Bad Thing: America was thus clearly top
nation and History came to a

Ib.

Robert W Service 1874-1958

96.2 This is the Law of the Yukon, that only the
Strong shall thrive;
That surely the Weak shall perish, and only
the Fit survive.

'The Law of the Yukon'

96.3 Back of the bar, in a solo game, sat
Dangerous Dan McGrew,
And watching his luck was his light o' love,
the lady that's known as Lou.

'The Shooting of Dan McGrew'

William Shakespere 1564-1616

96.4 My friends were poor but honest.

All's Well that Ends Well

96.5 The barge she sat in, like a burnished
throne,
Burned on the water; the poop was beaten
gold.

Anthony and Cleopatra

96.6 Age cannot wither her, nor custom stale
Her infinite variety.

Ib.

96.7 The bright day is done
And we are for the dark.

Ib.

97.1 Now boast thee death, in thy possession lies
A lass unparalleled.

Ib.

97.2 Sweet are the uses of adversity,
Which, like the toad, ugly and venomous,
Wears yet a precious jewel in his head;

As You Like It.

97.3 Under the greenwood tree
Who loves to lie with me.

Ib.

97.4 All the world's a stage,
And all the men and women merely players;
They have their exits and their entrances;
And one man in his time plays, many parts.

As You Like It

97.5 And then the whining school-boy, with his
satchel
And shining morning face, creeping like
snail
Unwilling to school.

Ib.

97.6 Boldness be my friend!

Cymbeline

98.1 Fear no more the heat o' the sun,
    Nor the furious winter's rages:
Thou thy worldy task hast done,
    Home art gone and ta'en thy wages:
Golden lads and girls all must,
    As chimney-sweepers, come to dust.

Ib

98.2 Neither a borrower nor a lender be;
For loan oft loses both itself and friend
And borrowing dulls the edge of husbandry.
This above all: to thine own self be true,
And it must follow, as night the day,
Thou canst not then be false to any man.

Hamlet

98.3 Something is rotten in the state of
Denmark.

Ib.

98.4 To be, or not to be: that is the question.

Hamlet

98.5 Alas! poor Yorick. I knew him, Horatio, a
fellow of excellent jest, of most excellent
fancy.

Ib.

98.6 The rest is silence.

Ib.

99.1 Now cracks a noble heart. Good-night, sweet
  prince,
And flights of angels sing thee to thy rest!

Ib.

99.2 If all the year were playing holidays,
To sport would be as tedious as to work.

Henry IV, Pt. 1

99.3 **Glendower:** I can call spirits from the
  vasty deep.
Hotspur: Why so can I, or so can any man;
But will they come when you do call for
  them?

Ib.

99.4 Uneasy lies the head that wears a crown.

Henry IV, Pt. 2

99.5 Now all the youth of England are on fire,
And silken dalliance in the wardrobe lies.

Henry V

99.6 His nose was a sharp as a pen, and a' babbled
of green fields.
(The death of Falstaff)

Ib.

99.7 Once more unto the breach, dear friends,
once more;

Ib.

100.1 Cry "God, for Harry! England and Saint
George!"

Ib.

100.2 Old men forget: yet all shall be forgot
But he'll remember with advantages
What feats he did that day.

Ib.

100.3 Let me have men about me that are fat;
Sleek-headed men and such as sleep
o' nights;
Yond Cassius has a lean and hungry look;
He thinks too much: such men are
dangerous

Julius Caesar

100.4 Let's carve him as a dish fit for the gods.

Ib.

100.5 Cowards die many times before their
deaths;
The valiant never taste of death but once.

Ib.

100.6 Et tu Brute.

Ib.

100.7 Cry 'Havoc!' and let slip the dogs of war.

Ib.

101.1 Friends, Romans, countrymen, lend me
       your ears:
       I come to bury Caesar, not to praise him.

Julius Caesar

101.2 For Brutus is an honourable man;
       So are they all, all honourable men.

Ib.

101.3 If you have tears, prepare to shed them
       now.

Ib.

101.4 There is a tide in the affairs of men,
       Which, taken at the flood, leads on to
       fortune.

Ib.

101.5 Why I will see thee at Philippi then.

Ib.

101.6 This was the noblest Roman of them all.

Ib.

101.7 The course of true love never did run
       smooth.

A Midsummer Night's Dream

101.8 Ill met by moonlight, proud Titania.

Ib.

102.1 I know a bank whereon the wild thyme
    blows,
Where oxlips and the nodding violet grows.

Ib.

102.2 Lord, what fools these mortals be!

Ib.

102.3 Is this a dagger which I see before me,
The handle toward my hand?

Macbeth

102.4 Out, damned spot! out, I say!

Ib.

102.5 Lay on, Macduff;
And damn'd be he that first cries, 'Hold,
    enough!'

Ib.

102.6 The quality of mercy is not strain'd.

The Merchant of Venice

102.7 There was a star danced, and under that
was I born.

Much Ado about Nothing

102.8 Sigh no more, ladies, sigh no more,
Men were deceivers ever.

Ib.

103.1 Comparisons are odorous.

Ib.

103.2 Now is the winter of our discontent.

Richard III

103.3 A horse! a horse! my kingdom for a horse.

Ib.

103.4 O! she doth teach the torches to burn
bright.

Romeo and Juliet

103.5 He jests at scars, that never felt a wound.

Ib.

103.6 Kiss me Kate!

The Taming of the Shrew

103.7 Full fathom five thy father lies
Of his bones are coral made.

The Tempest

103.8 Be not afeard: the isle is full of noises,
Sounds and sweet airs, that give delight
and hurt not.

Ib.

104.1 Our revels now are ended. These our actors,
As I foretold you, were all spirits and
Are melted into air, into thin air ...
       We are such stuff
As dreams are made on, and our little life
Is rounded with a sleep.

Ib.

104.2 If music be the food of love, play on.

Twelfth Night

104.3 Make me a willow cabin at your gate,
And call my soul within the house.

Ib.

104.4 Dost thou think because thou art virtuous,
there shall be no more cakes and ale.

Ib.

104.5 A sad tale's best for winter

The Winter's Tale

104.6 When icicles hang by the wall,
    And Dick the shepherd blows his nail,
And Tom bears logs into the hall,
    And milk comes frozen home in pail.

'Song' (Love's Labour's Lost)

'Elizabeth Shane' (Gertrude Hind) Early 20th Century

105.1 He's gone to school, Wee Hughie,
    An' him not four,
  Sure I saw the fright was in him
    When he left the door.

                      'Wee Hughie'

George Bernard Shaw 1856-1950

105.2 My aunt died of influenza; so they said ...
But it's my belief they done the old woman
in.

                      Pygmalion

105.3 Walk! Not bloody likely. I am going in a
taxi.

                      Ib.

General William Sherman 1820-1891

105.4 There is many a boy here today who looks on
war as all glory, but, boys it is all hell.

        Speech, Columbus, Ohio 11 August 1880

Emperor Sigismund 1361-1437

105.5 I am the Roman Emperor, and am above
grammar.

        Reply to clerygman who had criticised his Latin

Robert Southey 1774-1843

106.1   What are little girls made of ...?
        Sugar and spice and all things nice,
        And such are little girls made of.

'What All The World Is Made Of'

106.2   What are little boys made of, made of?
        What are little boys made of?
        Snips and snails and puppy-dogs tails,
        And such are little boys made of.

Ib.

Sir H M Stanley 1841-1904

106.3   Dr Livingstone, I presume.

How I Found Livingstone

James Stephens 1882-1950

106.4   I hear a sudden cry of pain!
        There is a rabbit in a snare.

'The Snare'

Robert Louis Stevenson 1850-1894

106.5   In winter I get up at night
        And dress by yellow candle-light.
        In summer, quite the other way,
        I have to go to bed by day.

'Bed in Summer'

107.1 Faster than fairies, faster than witches,
Bridges and houses, hedges and ditches;

'From a Railway Carriage'

107.2 The world is so full of a number of things,
I'm sure we should all be as happy as
kings.

'Happy Thought'

107.3 Under the wide and starry sky
Dig the grave and let me lie.
Glad did I live and gladly die,
    And I laid me down with a will.
This be the verse you grave for me:
'Here he lies where he longed to be;
Home is the hero, home from sea,
    And the hunter home for the hill.'

'Requiem'

107.4 Am I no a bonny fighter?

Kidnapped

107.5 Fifteen men on the dead man's chest—
Yo-yo-yo, and a bottle of rum!
Drink and the devil had done for the rest—

Treasure Island

107.6 Tip me the black spot.

Ib.

Abraham ('Bram') Stoker 1847-1912

108.1 The mouth, so far as I could see it under the heavy moustache, was fixed and rather cruel-looking, with peculiarly sharp white teeth; these protruded over the lips, whose remarkable ruddiness showed astonishing vitality in a man of his years.

Dracula

108.2 It was like a miracle; but before our very eyes, and almost in the drawing of a breath, the whole body crumbled into dust and passed from our sight.

Ib.

Sir John Suckling 1609-1642

108.3 Her feet beneath her petticoat,
Like little mice, stole in and out,
As if they feared the light.

'Upon a Wedding'

Suetonius c70-c140

108.4 Festina lente (Hasten slowly)

Augustus

108.5 Ave, Imperator, morituri te salutant (Hail, Emperor, those about to die salute you).

Claudius

Jonathan Swift 1667-1745

109.1 Instead of dirt and poison we have rather chosen to fill our hives with honey and wax; thus furnishing mankind with the two noblest of things, which are sweetness and light.

The Battle of the Books

109.2 And he gave it for his opinion, that whoever could make two ears of corn or two blades of grass to grow on a spot of ground where only one grew before, would deserve better of mankind, and do more essential service to his country than the whole race of politicians put together.

Gulliver's Travels

109.3 He had been eight years upon a project for extracting sunbeams out of cucumbers, which were to be put into phials hermetically sealed, and let out to warm the air in raw inclement summers.

Ib.

109.4 I have been assured by a very knowing American of my acquaintance in London, that a healthy child well nursed is at a year old a most delicious, nourishing, and a wholesome food, whether stewed, roasted, baked or boiled, and I make no doubt that it will equally serve in a fricassé or a ragout..

A Modest Proposal

Jane Taylor 1783-1824

110.1 Twinkle, twinkle, little star,
       How I wonder what you are!
       Up above the world, so high,
       Like a diamond in the sky.

'The Star' (See Lewis Carroll 25.1)

110.2 I like little pussy, her coat is so warm,
       And if I don't hurt her, she'll do me no harm.

'I like Little Pussy'

Alfred, Lord Tennyson 1809-1892

111.1 Cannon to the right of them,
    Cannon to the left of them,
    Cannon in front of them
       Volley'd and thunder'd.

'The Charge of the Light Brigade'

111.2   Come, my friends,
    'Tis not too late to seek a newer world.
    Push off, and sitting well in order smite
    The sounding furrows; for my purpose holds
    To sail beyond the sunset, and the baths
    Of all the western stars, until I die.

'Ulysses'

D'Arcy Wentworth Thompson 1829-1902

111.3 Who's that ringing at our door-bell?
    'I'm a little black cat, and I'm not very
       well.'
    'Then rub your little nose with a little
       mutton-fat,
    And that's the best cure for a little pussy
       cat.'

'The Little Black Cat'

Henry David Thoreau 1817-1862

111.4 The mass of men lead lives of quiet
    desperation.

Walden

112.1 Our life is frittered away by detail ... Simplify, simplify.

Ib.

112.2 Some circumstantial evidence is very strong, as when you find a trout in the milk.

Miscellanies

Mark Twain (Samuel Langhorne Clemens) 1835-1910

112.3 There was things which he stretched, but mainly he told the truth.

The Adventures of Huckleberry Finn

112.4 There was some books ... One was *Pilgrim's Progress* about a man that left his family, it didn't say why. I read considerable in it now and then. The statements was interesting but tough.

Ib.

112.5 There's plenty of boys that will come hankering and gruvelling around when you've got an apple, and beg the core off you; but when *they've* got one and you beg for the core and remind them how you give them a core one time, they make a mouth at you and say thenk you 'most to death, but there ain't-a-going to be no core.

Tom Sawyer Abroad

113.1 There ain't no way to find out why a snorer
        can't hear himself snore.

Ib.

113.2 A classic is something that everybody wants
        to have read and nobody wants to read.

The Disappearance of Literature

113.3 The report of my death was an exaggeration

Cable from Europe to the Press Association

Jules Verne 1828-1905

114.1 And to the question asked by Ecclesiastes 3000 years ago, "That which is far off and exceeding deep, who can find it out?" two men alone of all now living have the right to give an answer: Captain Nemo and Myself.

Twenty-Thousand Leagues Under the Sea

George Washington 1732-1799

115.1 Father, I cannot tell a lie. I did it with my
little hatchet.
When asked who cut down his father's cherry tree

Attrib.

Isaac Watts 1674-1748

115.2 Let dogs delight to bark and bite,
    For God hath made them so;
Let bears and lions growl and fight,
    For 'tis their nature too.

'Against Quarrelling'

115.3 Birds in their little nests agree.

'Love Between Brothers and Sisters'

116.1 In works of labour, or of skill,
        I would be busy too;
     For Satan finds some mischief still
        For idle hands to do.

'Against Idleness and Mischief'

Charles Wesley 1707-1788

116.2 Gentle Jesus, meek and mild,
        Look upon a little child;
     Pity my simplicity
        Suffer me to come to thee.

'Gentle Jesus, Meek and Mild'

116.3 Hark! the herald-angels sing
     Glory to the new-born King;
     Peace on earth, and mercy mild,
     God and sinners reconciled.

'Hark! the Herald Angels Sing'

Walt Whitman 1819-1892

116.4 Do I contradict myself?
     Very well then I contradict myself
     (I am large, I contain multitudes)

'Song of Myself'

Oscar Wilde 1856-1900

117.1 To lose one parent, Mr Worthing, may be
regarded as a misfortune; to lose both looks
like carelessness.

The Importance of Being Earnest

117.2 Cecily: When I see a spade I call it a spade.
Gwendolen: I am glad to say I have never
seen a spade. It is obvious that our social
spheres have been widely different.

Ib.

117.3 This suspense is terrible. I hope it will last.

Ib.

117.4 I never travel without my diary. One should
have always have something sensational to
read on the train.

Ib.

117.5 Is this Miss Prism a female of repellent
aspect, remotely connected with education?

Ib.

Philip Wingate fl 1894

117.6 You can't holler down our rain-bar'l
       You can't climb our apple-tree
    I don't want to play in your yard
       If you won't be good to me.

'I Don't Want to Play in Your Yard'

P G Wodehouse 1881-1975

118.1   If not actually disgruntled, he was far from
being gruntled.

The Code of the Woosters

Charles Wolfe 1791-1823

118.2   Not a drum was heard, not a funeral note,
As his corse to the rampart we hurried.

'The Burial of Sir John Moore'

118.3   He lay like a warrior taking his rest,
With his martial cloak around him.

Ib.

118.4   We carved not a line, and we raised not a
stone—
But we left him alone in his glory!

Ib.

William Wordsworth 1770-1850

118.5   I wandered lonely as a cloud
That floats on high o'er vales and hills,
When all at once I saw a crowd,
A host, of golden daffodils.

'The Daffodils'

118.6   The rainbow comes and goes,
And lovely is the rose.

'Ode. Intimations of Immortality'

119.1 Heaven lies about us in our infancy!
Shades of the prison house begin to close
Upon the growing boy.

Ib.

119.2 Bliss was it in that dawn to be alive
But to be young was very heaven!

The Prelude

119.3 Breaking the silence of the sea
Among the farthest Hebrides.

'The Solitary Reaper'

119.4 For old, unhappy, far-off things,
And battles long ago.

Ib.

119.5 I have learned
To look on nature, not as in the hour of
thoughtless youth; but hearing oftentimes
The still, sad music of humanity,
Nor harsh nor grating, though of ample
power
To chasten and subdue.

'Tintern Abbey'

William Butler Yeats 1865-1939

120.1 Down by the salley gardens my love and I
          did meet;
       She passed the salley gardens with little
          snow-white feet.
       She bid me take love easy, as the leaves
          grow on the tree;
       But I, being young and foolish, with her
          would not agree.

'Down by the Salley Gardens'

120.2 All changed, changed utterly:
       A terrible beauty is born.

'Easter 1916'

121.1 When I play on my fiddle in Dooney
Folk dance like a wave of the sea.

'The Fiddler of Dooney'

121.2 I will arise and go now, and go to Innisfree,
And a small cabin build there, of clay and
wattles made.

'The Lake Isle of Innisfree'

121.3 And pluck till time and times are done
The silver apples of the moon
The golden apples of the sun.

'The Song of Wandering Aengus'

121.4 May she become a flourishing hidden tree
That all her thoughts may like the linnet be.

'A Prayer for My Daughter'

121.5 If there's no hatred in a mind
Assault and battery of the wind
Can never tear the linnet from the leaf.

'A Prayer for My Daughter'

Andrew Young 1807-1889

121.6 There is a happy land,
Far, far away,
Where Saints in glory stand
Bright, bright as day.

'There Is a Happy Land'

Emile Zola 1840-1902

122.1 *J'accuse*

Title of an open letter to the French President concerning the Dreyfus case, 1898.

Zozimus, (Michael Moran) 1794-1846

122.2 Saint Patrick was a gintleman, he came of decent people,
In Dublin town he built a church, and upon't put a steeple;
His father was a Callaghan, his mother was a Brady,
His aunt was an O'Shaughnessy, his uncle was a Grady.

'Saint Patrick Was A Gentleman'

The Holy Bible

123.1 In the beginning God created the heaven and the earth.

Genesis

123.2 And he dreamed, and behold a ladder set up on the earth, and the top of it reached to heaven: and behold the angels of God ascending and descending on it. (Jacob)

Ib.

123.3 I am that I am.

Exodus

124.1 Life for life
Eye for eye, tooth for tooth, hand for hand,
  foot for foot,
Burning for burning, wound for wound,
  stripe for stripe.

Ib.

124.2 There ariseth a little cloud out of the sea,
like a man's hand.

1 Kings

124.3 Man is born unto trouble, as the sparks fly
upward.

Job

124.4 He that spareth the rod hateth his son.

Proverbs

124.5 As a dog returneth to his vomit, so a fool
returneth to his folly.

Ib.

124.6 To every thing there is a season, and a time
to every purpose under heaven:

A time to weep, and a time to laugh; a time
to mourn, and a time to dance.

Ecclesiastes

124.7 Of making many books there is no end; and
much study is a weariness of the flesh.

Ib.

125.1 Stay me with flagons, comfort me with apples.

The Song of Solomon

125.2 Rise up, my love, my fair one, and come
away.
For, lo, the winter is past, the rain is over
and gone;
The flowers appear on the earth; the time of
the singing birds is come, and the voice of
the turtle is heard in the land.

Ib.

125.3 Behold, a virgin shall conceive, and bear a
son, and shall call his name Immanuel.

Isaiah

125.4 Let us eat and drink; for tomorrow we shall
die.

Ib.

125.5 The fathers have eaten sour grapes, and the
children's teeth are set on edge.

Ezekiel

125.6 Blessed are the poor in spirit: for theirs is
the kingdom of heaven.

St Matthew

126.1 And there were in the same country shepherds abiding in the field, keeping watch over their flock by night. And, lo, the angel of the Lord came upon them, and the glory of the Lord shone about them: and they were sore afraid.

St Luke

126.2 The sabbath was made for man, and not man for the sabbath.

St Mark

126.3 In the beginning was the Word, and the Word was with God, and the Word was God.

St John

126.4 When I was a child, I spake as a child, I understood as a child, I thought as a child; but when I became a man, I put away childish things.

1 Corinthians

126.5 Though I speak with the tongues of men and of angels, and have not charity, I am become as sounding brass, or a tinkling cymbal.

Ib.

126.6 God loveth a cheerful giver.

2 Corinthians

127.1 I am Alpha and Omega, the beginning and ending, saith the Lord.

Revelation

127.2 And I looked, and behold, a pale horse: and his name that sat on him was Death.

Ib.

Subject Index

Book(s), 11.2; 14.3; 15.2;
36.1; 86.2; 112.4; 124.7
Borrower, 98.2
Boundary, 85.1
Bow, 4.3; 16.5
Boy(s), 36.1; 53.2; 63.1;
105.4
Boycott, 84.2
Brass: sounding brass,
126.5
Bright, 17.2; 96.7; 103.4;
121.6
British, 71.3
British Empire, 28.4
Buckingham Palace, 74.4
Bug, 44.3
Buns, 5.1
Burial, 118.2; 118.3; 118.4
Burning, 124.1
Butter, 25.3

Cabbages, 26.1
Cabin, 104.3; 121.2
Caesar, 101.1
Cakes, 72.4; 104.4
Calculators, 20.5
Cambridge, 18.4
Candle, 66.2;
candle-light, 6.1
Cannon, 34.3; 111.1
Captain, 45.2; 53.4
Caravan, 91.2
Cat, 8.1
Changeling, 74.2
Chariot, 16.5
Charity, 126.5
Cherry-tree, 57.3
Chicken(s), 2.1

Child, 6.4; 109.4; 116.2;
125.5
childish things, 126.4
Chimney-sweep, 98.1
Chivalry, 21.5
Christian, 12.2
Christmas, 76.1
Church, 18.5
Churchyard, 49.4
Classic, 113.2
Clay, 121.2
Clock, 18.5
Clothes, 3.4
Cloud(s), 16.5; 118.5; 124.2
Cock Robin, 4.3
Colonel, 37.1
Conflict, 29.1
Constellations, 51.3
Contradict, 116.4
Cook, 45.2
Coral, 103.7
Cormorant, 5.1
Corn, 109.2
Country, 33.3; 41.2; 81.3;
85.1; 109.2
Cow(s), 20.1; 62.1
Cowards, 100.5
Creatures great & small, 2.5
Cricket, 58.5; 80.1; 80.2
Crime, 87.3
Cross, 12.2; 30.6
Crown, 99.4
Crucified, 2.6
Crumbs, 5.1
Cucumbers, 109.2
Custom, 96.6

Daffodils, 118.5

Fire(s), 43.4; 53.5
Fish, 5.2
Flagons, 125.1
Fleas, 34.4
Flesh, 35.5; 124.7
Flock, 126.1
Flower(s), 50.2; 54.1; 125.2
Fly, 58.1
Folly, 124.5
Food, 104.2; 109.4
Fool(s), 63.2; 86.5; 102.2;
    124.5
Foot, 124.1
Footprints, 69.2
Fortune, 101.4
Fought, 61.3
Fox, 1.2; 1.3
France, 20.4; 78.2
French, 78.2
Free, 61.3; 63.3
Freedom, 59.1; 61.2; 68.3
Frog, 5.3
Funeral, 118.2
Funny, 52.5

Gallant, 95.2
Game, 31.2; 58.5; 80.2; 92.1;
    96.3
Garden, 50.6
Gaul, 22.1
Genius, 39.1
Gentleman, 122.2
Geography, 15.4
Ghost, 87.5
Girl(s), 23.3; 70.1; 106.1
Giver, 126.6
Glen, 3.1
Glory, 50.1; 57.5; 83.1; 87.4;

    105.4; 116.3; 118.4;
    121.6; 126.1
    glorious life, 77.4
God, 16.2; 27.3; 33.2; 34.2;
    50.6; 54.4; 66.2; 68.3;
    68.4; 70.5; 115.2; 123.1;
    126.3; 126.6
Gods, 100.4
Gold, 96.5
Good, 55.1; 70.1
Goodness, 55.1
Governess, 67.2
Government, 68.3
Grace, 66.2
Grammar, 105.5
Grandeur, 87.4
Grapes, 1.2
    sour grapes, 125.5
Grass, 109.2
Grave(s), 50.1; 73.4; 86.5;
    107.3
Graveyard, 14.1
Gravy, 15.5
Greatness, 20.3
Greece, 87.4
Green, 2.6; 17.1; 17.4
Ground, 109.2

Hair, 4.1; 5.4
Hand, 124.1; 124.2
Hang, Hanging, 23.4; 44.2;
    87.2; 92.2
Happy, 107.2; 121.6
Harp, 76.4; 77.2
Hatchet, 115.1
Hatred, 121.5
Head, 99.4
Hearse, 4.1

131

132

Lean, 100.3
Lender, 98.2
Lever, 9.4
Lie(s),14.5; 115.1
Liberty, 59.1
Life, 32.2; 69.2; 89.5; 112.1
Light, 4.2; 26.3; 29.2; 109.1
   light fantastic, 57.5
Lightning, 5.1; 37.5
Lighthouse, 5.2
Linnet, 121.4
Lions, 115.2
Lips, 108.1
Llama, 79.2
Loch Lomond, 6.3
Lonely, 118.5
Lord, 2.5; 2.6; 57.5; 127.1
Lord God, 2.5
Louse, 21.4
Love, 101.7; 104.2; 120.1

Man, 7.1; 9.5; 27.2; 32.1;
   33.5; 47.3; 126.2; 126.4
   Man Friday, 34.1
   single man, 10.1
   young man, 87.3
Mankind, 9.5
March, 27.4
March Hare, 25.3
Marksmen, 90.1
Mask, 37.5
Master, 53.4
Match, 80.1
Matrimony, 89.3
Maypole, 4.4
Melodeon, 62.1
Memory, 41.2; 77.3
Men, 21.5; 27.3; 29.5; 30.2;

59.1; 90.1; 102.8; 111.4
Mercy, 23.1; 102.6; 116.3
Mermaid, 5.2
Merry, 4.1; 17.4
Mice, 8.1; 14.2; 21.5; 108.3
Miles, 6.1
Milk, 112.2
Mind, 121.5
Miner, 75.4
Minstrel boy, 77.2
Miracle, 108.2
Mischief, 7.1; 43.5; 116.1
Misery, 89.4
Misfortune, 117.1
Mist, 30.3
Monday's child, 6.4
Montezuma, 71.1
Months, 48.1
Moon, 26.3; 121.3
Moonlight, 87.5; 101.8
Morality, 71.3
Mortals, 102.2
Mother, 6.2
   Mother Hubbard, 7.3
Mountain, 3.1
Mourn, 124.6
Mouse, 21.5
Mouth, 108.1
Mud, 66.1
Music, 30.4; 76.4; 82.3;
   104.2; 119.5

Nation, 33.1; 41.2; 85.1
Native land, 61.3; 94.4
Nativity, 126.1
Nature, 119.5
Naughty, 63.1
Nests, 115.3

Acknowledgements

For kind permission to reproduce copyright material, the publishers gratefully acknowledge the following:

Century Publishers for the extract from *Borstal Boy* by Brendan Behan; Duckworth and Co Ltd for "Henry King", "Matilda" and the dedication to *Bad Child's Book of Beasts,* from *The Complete Verse of Hilaire Belloc*; the Irish Writers' Union for lines from "A Cradle Song" and "An Old Woman of the Roads" by Padraic Colum; the executors of the James Joyce estate and Jonathan Cape Ltd for the extract from *The Portrait of the Artist as a Young Man* by James Joyce; the estate of Patrick Kavanagh, c/o Peter Fallon, Loughcrew, Oldcastle, Co Meath for lines from "A Christmas Childhood" by Patrick Kavanagh; The Society of Authors as the literary representative of the estate of John Masefield for lines from "Sea Fever;" Faber and Faber Ltd for "Ancient Music" by Ezra Pound; The Society of Authors on behalf of the Bernard Shaw estate for the extracts from *Pygmalion* by George Bernard Shaw;

Every attempt had been made to contact the copyright holders and Poolbeg Press apologises for any errors or omissions in the above list. The editor and publishers would be grateful to be notified of any corrections that should be incorporated in future editions of this book.

Children's POOLBEG

Orla Was Six			*Brogeen and the Green*	
Mary Beckett	£2.99		*Shoes*	
Candy on the Dart			Patricia Lynch	£3.50
Ita Daly	£2.99		*Patsy-O*	
When the Luvenders			Bryan MacMahon	£2.99
Came to Merrick Town			*Growing Things*	
June Considine	£3.50		Sean McCann	£2.99
Discoveries			*Shoes and Ships and*	
Clodagh Corcoran ed	£4.99		*Sealing-Wax*	
Baker's Dozen			*A Book of Quotations for Children*	
Clodagh Corcoran ed	£3.50		Sean McMahon ed	£2.99
Children's Quiz Book No. 1			*The Poolbeg Book of*	
Robert Duffy	£2.99		*Children's Verse*	
Children's Quiz Book No. 2			Sean McMahon ed	£4.95
Robert Duffy	£2.99		*The Viking Princess*	
Joe in the Middle			Michael Mullen	£2.99
Tony Hickey	£2.99		*The Little Drummer Boy*	
Where is Joe?			Michael Mullen	£2.99
Tony Hickey	£3.50		*The Little Black Hen*	
Spike and the Professor			Eileen O'Faoláin	£2.99
Tony Hickey	£2.99		*An Nollaig Thiar*	
Blanketland			Breandán Ó hEithir	£2.99
Tony Hickey	£2.99		*Bugsy Goes to Limerick*	
The Bridge of Feathers			Carolyn Swift	£2.99
Eamon Kelly	£2.99		*Robbers on TV*	
The Turf-Cutter's Donkey			Carolyn Swift	£2.99
Patricia Lynch	£2.99		*A Little Man in England*	
Brogeen Follows the			Shaun Traynor	£2.99
Magic Tune			*Hugo O'Huge*	
Patricia Lynch	£2.99		Shaun Traynor	£2.99

The Poolbeg Book of
Children's Verse

Edited by Sean McMahon

A sparkling miscellany of poems for the
young and everybody else.

"Already a classic,"
RTE Guide

POOLBEG

Irish Sagas and Folk Tales

by Eileen O'Faoláin

Here is a classic collection of tales
from the folklore of Ireland

POOLBEG